A Poetic Biography
Albert Russo
Biographie Poétique

by / par
Eric Tessier

To order additional copies of this book, contact:
Xlibris
1-888-795-4274
www.Xlibris.com
Orders@Xlibris.com

ISBN: 978-1-5992-6871-2 (sc)
ISBN: 978-1-5992-6872-9 (hc)

Library of Congress Control Number: 2005908833

Print information available on the last page

Rev. date: 10/29/2019

2

Father came by boat, a stowaway,
A smile and a flannel suit were his only fortune
He came to conquer Africa

Père est venu par bateau, passager clandestin
Un sourire et un costume de flanelle en guise de fortune
Il allait conquérir l'Afrique

3

Mother came by plane
She walked the tarmac, England in her heart
and dreams in her head

Mère est venue par avion
Elle foula la piste, l'Angleterre dans son cœur
des rêves pleins la tête

He was from RHODES
She grew up in RHODESia
They were meant to meet

Il venait de RHODES
Elle grandit en RHODESie
Ils étaient faits pour se rencontrer

Congo – heart of darkness
What was your most thrilling challenge?
Running the jungle or raising a family?

Congo – cœur d'ébène
Quel était ton défi le plus excitant?
Courir la jungle ou fonder une famille?

The formidable challenge of writing a book
after a long and patient,
often excruciating gestation

Le seul défi qui vaille pour un auteur: un livre
qui n'est que le résultat d'une longue, patiente,
et souvent douloureuse gestation

The sensuality of your body
reflected in a silver tray
I stare at you, dazzled

La sensualité de ton corps
réfléchie dans un plateau d'argent
et moi, ébloui

Dressed to kill
a fragrance of musk and vetiver
I look on, gratefully

Sapé comme un milord
Ton parfum, fort, enivrant
et moi, ému

Africa – a continent for adventurers
They were ready to endure everything
and everything seemed possible

Afrique – un continent pour les aventuriers
Ils étaient prêts à tout endurer
et tout semblait possible

I loved the quietness of the city
its majesty and its inhabitants
its long hot afternoons

J'aimais le calme de la ville
sa majesté et ses habitants
ses longs après-midi ensoleillés

A house on the hill
under the warm African sun
facing lake Tanganyika

Une maison à flanc de colline
sous le chaud soleil d'Afrique
faisant face au lac Tanganyika

Riding my bicycle to go to school
down the hill – the going was easy
Coming back was harder

Je prenais mon vélo pour aller à l'école
en bas de la colline – l'aller était facile
Le retour beaucoup plus dur

Weekends were occasions to drive around
Majestic, imposing, the car was a cruiser
Queen of the road

Les dimanches étaient prétextes à de longues ballades
Majestueuse, imposante, la voiture tanguait comme un paquebot
Reine de la route

Switzerland – Astonishing holidays
how far from Katanga
and its luxuriant flora!

La Suisse – des vacances étonnantes
si loin du Katanga
et de sa flore luxuriante!

15

A sound in the air, so fragile
Ephemeral, music notes go fluttering every which way,
Why do the strings hurt my fingers so badly?

Un son dans l'espace, si fragile
La musique vole, éphémère et libre
Pourquoi des cordes si râpeuses sous mes doigts?

From Burundi to Brooklyn
From horizontality to verticality
Africa forever in my heart

Du Burundi à Brooklyn
De l'horizontal au vertical
L'Afrique à jamais dans mon cœur

New York city – the first poems
Between NYU and the Village
Still fragile, creation appears

EXPECTANCY
by Albert Russo

there's a world at peace and there's a world at war
the frontiers between the two shift and overlap
like waves over the breakers at low tide
and as you watch the evening news
you feel your heart skitter across the water
on the safe side, or so you will yourself to believe
but when in the dead of night you switch off the bedlamp
the rumblings under your skin
at first distant and familiar
start sending out portentous signals
then, somewhere around the solar plexus
there's an expectancy of pain
searing as the alarm caused by a misfired thunder
it shoots through the arteries to the cortex
making the flesh quiver in its wake
and suddenly the echo of a reverberating crackle
turns your entire body into an electric web
so tightly packed you instinctively
embrace all the destructive power
of mankind's folly

New York – les premiers poèmes
Entre l'université et Greenwich Village
Encore fragile, apparaît la création

The first two years in this concrete jungle
had been awful. Two worlds collided.
Where was my beloved savanna?

Les deux premières années dans cette jungle de béton
furent horribles. Deux mondes se percutaient.
Où était ma savane bien aimée?

But I've come to love The Big Apple
Leaving Brooklyn, I discovered
New York was a mosaic

Mais j'appris à aimer la Grosse Pomme
En quittant Brooklyn, j'ai découvert
la fabuleuse mosaïque newyorkaise

Writers, painters, pranksters,
we were a bunch of young creators
The world was ours

Peintres, poètes, plaisantins,
nous étions une bande de jeunes créateurs
Le monde nous appartenait

Two authors, two brothers
An African American writes to a Belgian African:
"You're a dangerous man" - reciprocal admiration

Dear Albert Russo :

I am sorry to have taken so long to anwer you, but I have been busy, and a trifle ill - actually, I think more exhausted than ill but doctors can be very boring. Anyway, I'm back at the type-writer.

I've read everything you sent me, and I like your work very much indeed. It has a very gentle surface and a savage under-tow - the fiction - and I applaud the wicked portrait of Ionesco. You're a dangerous man.

I don't doubt the general publishing reaction to your work. You are saying something, after all, which no-one particularly wants to hear and saying it, furthermore, from a particularly intimidating point of view.

With your permission, however, I might send the excerpts you have sent me on to a friend of mine, at Random House, in New York. My friend is the Black woman novelist, Toni Morrison, who is an editor there. She is, in every way, beautiful, extraordinary, swift, and knows what you are talking about. Or you can send whatever you want, using my name, and I'll warn her to expect to hear from you.

Let me know how you want to handle it, and we'll see what happens. (You might wish to send a broader collection.)

I'm in Paris on the 24th of this month and hope to see you. My phone, here : (93) 32 87 90.

all the best,

James Baldwin

Deux auteurs, deux frères
Un Africain Américain écrit à un Belge Africain:
"Vous êtes un homme dangereux" - admiration réciproque

Belgium – first publication in French
"I'll publish everything you write", said Pierre Deméyère
And then a TV show

Belgique – première publication en français
"Je publierai tout ce que vous écrirez", dit Pierre Deméyère
Et puis, une émission de télévision

23

1992 – signing a book in Paris
A magnificent and acute description of apartheid
Banned in South Africa

1992 – signature dans une librairie parisienne
Une description formidable et acérée de l'apartheid
Interdit en Afrique du Sud

The dreamland that was daddy's store:
Toys, candies, dresses, lamps...
Useful or not, whatever you wished to buy, it was there

La caverne d'Ali Baba, le magasin de papa :
Jouets, bonbons, robes, lampes...
Utiles ou non, tout ce que vous désiriez était là

Dancing in the sun
with the pride of an ancient descendant
Nobility in their eyes

Ils dansent dans le soleil
avec la fierté d'une ancienne lignée
Quelle noblesse dans leurs yeux!

Graduation day
Elisabethville's high society
Applauding its most deserving children

Remise des prix de fin d'année scolaire
La haute société d'Elisabethville
venait applaudir ses enfants les plus méritants

Clerks, truck drivers and accountants
The little store had become an important firm
whose boss was no longer "that poor boy from Rhodes"

Vendeurs, conducteurs de camion et un comptable
Le modeste magasin était devenu une entreprise importante
et le "petit garçon pauvre de Rhodes" était maintenant un notable

Beauty of the models
A touch of Africa, a touch of Europe
Women from Usumbura were discussing the new dresses for hours

La beauté des mannequins
pour une mode à moitié africaine, à moitié européenne
Pendant des heures, les femmes d'Usumbura discutaient des nouvelles robes sorties

Running the world
Goggle-eyed tourist
hungry for beauty

Courir le monde
en touriste passionné
assoiffé de beauté

Running the world
Fearless businessmen
but the writer protests

Courir le monde
en intrépides hommes d'affaire
mais l'écrivain proteste

Citizen of the world, that's my claim
"Dirty Jew!", spat out the cripple-minded morons
That's how I became a Jewish citizen of the world

Je me revendique Citoyen du monde
"Sale Juif! ", crachèrent des demeurés à l'esprit atrophié
C'est ainsi que je devins un Juif Citoyen du monde

Graduation day: somebody stole our gowns
The ceremony couldn't be cancelled
So, we made do with what we found

Remise des diplômes: quelqu'un avait volé les toges
Impossible d'annuler la cérémonie
Nous fîmes avec ce que nous trouvâmes

Father – I did my best
but I wasn't a money man
just a man of letters

Le père – J'ai fait de mon mieux
mais je n'étais pas un homme d'argent
juste un homme de lettres

Daughter – mentioning it sounds easy:
UCSD and Sciences-Po, in Paris
London School of Economics… and a beaming smile

La fille – ça a l'air si simple:
Université de San Diego, en Californie, et Sciences-Po à Paris
London School of Economics… et un sourire épanoui

Summertime in Paris, 95°
Along the boulevards with a friend
Laughs and ice creams – paradise!

Un été à Paris, 35° à l'ombre
En flânant sur les boulevards avec un ami
Des rires et des glaces – le paradis!

Summertime, Rockefeller Center, NYC, 104°
Implacable, the sun above our heads
Nothing beats a drink of cool water

Un été à New York, Rockefeller Center, 40° à l'ombre
Implacable au-dessus de nos têtes, le soleil
Rien ne vaut une bonne gorgée d'eau fraîche

In front of Radio City Music Hall, NYC
The Rockettes began here
in Usa, Rwanda-Urundi

Avant de remplir le Radio City Music Hall à New York
Les Rockettes ont commencé ici
Usa, Rwanda-Urundi

First vacation in a lifetime
Paris 1950, the city of light
(re)discovering Europe

Premières vacances de toute une vie
Paris 1950, la ville-lumière
A la (re)découverte de l'Europe

"Choose your language", quipped an Argentinian writer living in France
But for a bilingual author, with a multicultural background,
the injunction is nonsensical: "Why would I restrict my writing?"

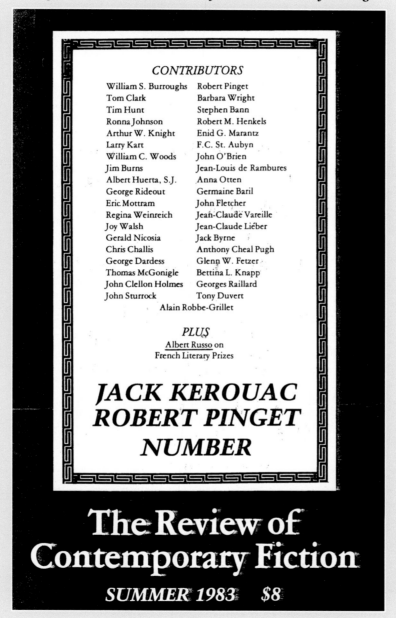

CONTRIBUTORS

William S. Burroughs	Robert Pinget
Tom Clark	Barbara Wright
Tim Hunt	Stephen Bann
Ronna Johnson	Robert M. Henkels
Arthur W. Knight	Enid G. Marantz
Larry Kart	F.C. St. Aubyn
William C. Woods	John O'Brien
Jim Burns	Jean-Louis de Rambures
Albert Huerta, S.J.	Anna Otten
George Rideout	Germaine Baril
Eric Mottram	John Fletcher
Regina Weinreich	Jean-Claude Vareille
Joy Walsh	Jean-Claude Liéber
Gerald Nicosia	Jack Byrne
Chris Challis	Anthony Cheal Pugh
George Dardess	Glenn W. Fetzer
Thomas McGonigle	Bettina L. Knapp
John Clellon Holmes	Georges Raillard
John Sturrock	Tony Duvert

Alain Robbe-Grillet

PLUS
Albert Russo on
French Literary Prizes

JACK KEROUAC
ROBERT PINGET
NUMBER

The Review of
Contemporary Fiction

SUMMER 1983 $8

"Vous devez choisir votre langue", dit un écrivain argentin vivant en France
Mais pour un auteur bilingue, élevé dans un environnement multiculturel
l'injonction n'a aucun sens: "Pourquoi restreindre mon écriture?"

Spain, Rhodes, The Congo and Rhodesia
Italy, South Africa and Montgomery, Alabama
Is the world wide enough for the family?

Espagne, Rhodes, Congo et Rhodésie
Italie, Afrique du Sud et Montgomery, en Alabama
Le monde est-il assez vaste pour la famille?

"Back in the USSR", sang the Beatles
This, however, was East Germany, by the Wall
"Ich habe my Herz in Heidelberg verloren"

"Back in the USSR", chantaient les Beatles
Nous étions juste en RDA, près du Mur.
"Ich habe my Herz in Heidelberg verloren"

Iowa city – Doris and Jackie
A literary seminar
A most memorable week in the Midwest

Iowa city – Doris et Jackie
Un séminaire littéraire
Une semaine exceptionnelle dans le Midwest

WORLD LITERATURE TODAY

A Literary Quarterly of the University of Oklahoma
Founded as *Books Abroad* in 1927

Djelal Kadir, Editor/Director and
Neustadt Professor of Comparative Literature

Mr. Albert Russo
BP 640
75826 Paris Cedex 17
FRANCE

{ email: zapinet@worldnet.fr
{ http://www.worldnet.net/~zapinet

Via Telefax: 33.01.47.66.44.59

Dear Mr. Russo:

I write to invite you to join us here in Oklahoma next year between March 27 and 30, 1996 as a member of the jury for the Neustadt International Prize for Literature. The Neustadt Prize is one of the most prestigious prizes in the world, with eighteen of our laureates, candidates, or jurors in the last twenty-five years having gone on to win the Nobel Prize following their affiliation with the Neustadt .

The twelve jurors from around the world will travel to Norman, Oklahoma on March 27, 1996 and engage in deliberations on the 28th and 29th, with a banquet honoring the jury the evening of the 30th. We shall cover all of your transportation expenses and furnish accommodations and hospitality. While we can not pay honoraria to the jurors, each juror, of course, has the possibility to garner the $40,000 prize for his or her candidate. Each juror nominates a candidate far enough in advance so that we may gather a representative selection of each candidate's materials for distribution to all the jurors prior to their arrival here. Writers working in any language are eligible for nomination and the candidate's work—fiction, poetry, or drama—should be available in English and French or Spanish, the languages usually shared by the jurors. The nominee should be able and willing to travel here for the award ceremony a few months after the jury has announced its decision. Since *World Literature Today* and the Neustadt Prize aim at truly international standards in the evaluation of contemporary world literature, jurors are not restricted in any way to offering candidates from their own country or language area. Should you yourself emerge as a candidate in the nomination process, your candidacy will take precedence over your role as juror, of course.

I am very hopeful that we shall have the privilege of having you with us as a juror next March and I look forward to hearing from you at your earliest convenience to that effect. As I am about to leave for an extended period at the end of August, I hope to have your response at the earliest date possible and hopefully prior to my departure. In the meantime, I remain

Yours, sincerely,

Djelal Kadir

110 Monnet Hall, University of Oklahoma, Norman, Oklahoma 73019-0375, USA
Phone: (405) 325-4531 Fax: (405) 325-7495 e-mail: djk@wlt.uoknor.edu

*London, England, a juror no more
but a laureate
of the British Diversity Award*

*Londres, Angleterre, ce n'est pas le juré
cette fois-ci, mais le lauréat
du British Diversity Award*

A man of words
A man of worlds
Sri Lanka took me in its arms

Un homme de mots
Un homme de mondes
Le Sri Lanka m'a accueilli

Different languages
for the same place
and the same man

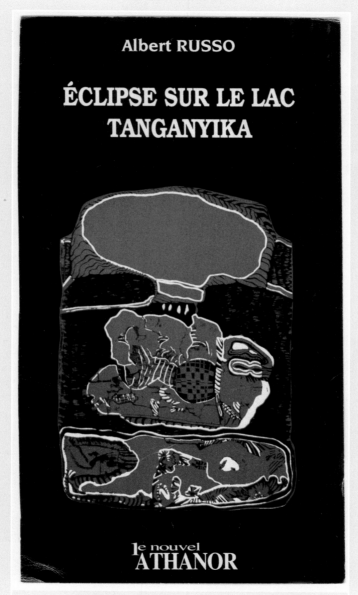

Des langues différentes
pour un même endroit
et un même homme

ALBERT RUSSO

Schemering over het Tanganjika-meer

ROMAN OVER HUTU'S EN TUTSI'S

ELEMENT

*Des langues différentes
pour l'amour de l'Afrique
inoubliable, inoubliée*

49

Tenderness
Warmth and happiness
A moment in time

Tendresse
Chaleur, bonheur
Un moment à deux

Complicity
Is the teacher competent?
I don't know but we are having fun

Complicité
Le professeur est-il compétent?
En tout cas, on rigole bien

Family as one entity
Each generation is a link
in a never-ending chain

La famille comme entité
Chaque génération est un lien
dans une chaîne sans fin

Each person is a link
between past and future
Our future is already our children's past

Chaque personne est un lien
entre le passé et le futur
Notre futur est déjà le passé de nos enfants

Jadotville, 1946, award of merit
A time fracture. It could have been 1988
somewhere in the UK

a Jadothville (congo Belge)

Mois de Ier trimestre 1946

Carte d'Honneur

méritée par   Albert Russo

qui a obtenu _____ bonnes notes sur _____

Jadotville, 1946, carte d'honneur
Fracture du temps, ça aurait pu être 1988
quelque part au Royaume-Uni

Award of merit
like an echo of childhood
A little ecstasy

AWARD OF MERIT CERTIFICATE

Presented to: __ALBERT RUSSO__

For Poem __'SOLILOQUY'__

Rank __DISTINCTION__ Category __ECSTASY__ Date __MAY 1988__

In Appreciation _____

D. MURPHY-GIBB, T. DuQUESNE, C. MORGAN

THE YEATS CLUB

P.O. BOX 271   OXFORD OX 26 DU

Mireille, we used to play in the garden.
You were always laughing
Gorgeous in the heat of the summer

Mireille, nos jeux complices
Ta bonne humeur, ta brusquerie parfois
Superbe dans la chaleur du mois de décembre

Africa – a continent for adventurers
I was ready to face everything
even an army of ladybugs

Afrique – un continent pour les aventuriers
J'étais prêt à tout affronter
même une armée de coccinelles

Ink from my pen,
typewriter ribbon or printer cartridge
this is my blood

Masking Shadows

Lassitude of being alive haunts the fellow next door
I can read it on his half moons
whenever he walks down the street
He hates running errands
but that is the sole thread which links him to life
or the semblance of it
When our eyes meet he gives me a quick nod
even that gesture is painstaking
never accompanied by a smile
for a smile might bare a corner of his soul
and that may be the most dangerous
most lurid place in a human being
'tis where small crimes are committed
without the cognizance of strangers
where one's own shadows become treacherous
it is a spot fraught with mystery and chimerae

by Albert Russo

Encre du stylo, du ruban de la machine à écrire
ou de la cartouche d'imprimante
c'est mon sang

Mother's Day: from the inkpot
came the words of love
Children write the most beautiful poems

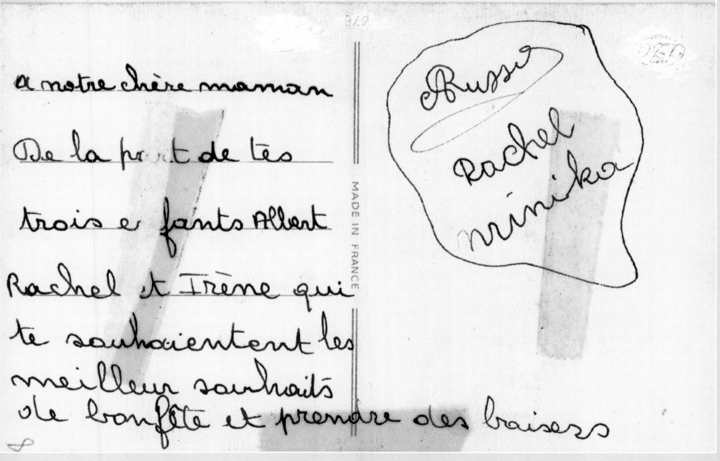

Fête des mères: de l'encrier
sortent les mots de l'amour
Ce sont les enfants qui écrivent les plus magnifiques poèmes

Zapinette, what a pest,
you're the limit!
That's why we love you

Albert Russo

ZAPINETTE VIDÉO

HC
Editions
Hors Commerce

Roman

Zapinette, insupportable petite peste
Insolente et admirable d'acuité
Si tonton m'était conté…

I work so hard
I write and write and rewrite
and the trashcan is full of drafts

Je travaille dur
J'écris, écris et réécris
si bien que la poubelle déborde de brouillons

Childhood is never far away
Never to be forgotten
As for me, it's on my desk

L'enfance n'est jamais très loin
On ne doit jamais l'oublier
En ce qui me concerne, la mienne est sur mon bureau

When I'm a grown-up
I'll buy tons of toys
for my place to be a toddler's dream

Quand je serai grand
je m'achèterai des tonnes de jouets
que ma maison soit un rêve d'enfant

Father didn't want his son to be a writer
Our name appears now between prestigious covers
What would he think of it?

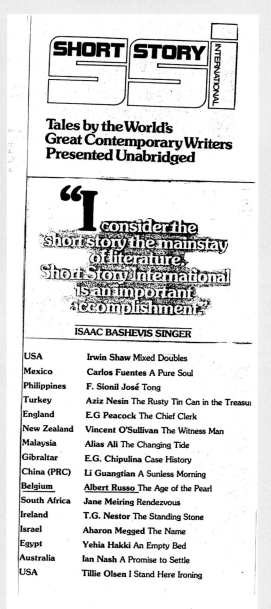

Le père ne voulait pas que le fils soit écrivain
Notre nom, désormais, est inscrit sur les affiches les plus prestigieuses
Qu'en penserait-il?

Spring in an Italian garden
Flowers like colorful waves
of an enchanted sea

Printemps dans un jardin italien
Les fleurs comme les vagues colorées
d'une mer enchantée

What time is it?
The cuckoo clock is an open door
leading to the real world – a world full of wonders

Quelle heure est-il?
Le coucou est une porte ouverte
sur la vraie réalité – le rêve

DC 7, DC 10, Constellation.
Flying over the humdrum of everyday life
My observation deck

DC 7, DC 10, Constellation
Survoler la vie quotidienne
Une façon de prendre du recul

Registering and codifying,
stamping and classifying
Redtape reigns

CONGO BELGE
BELGISCH KONGO

PROVINCE .du .Katanga...............   Nº ..I459.....
PROVINCIE ....   Nr ....
DISTRICT .du .Haut-Katanga.........
DISTRICT ....

ATTESTATION DELIVREE A L'EPOUSE ET AUX ENFANTS MINEURS
DU TITULAIRE DU CERTIFICAT DE RESIDANT PERMANENT
GETUIGSCHRIFT AFGEGEVEN AAN DE ECHTGENOTE EN DE MINDERJARIGE
KINDEREN VAN DE HOUDER VAN HET BEWIJS VAN PERMANENT RESIDENT

L'Administrateur du Territoire de ....
De Gewestbeheerder van het Gewest
Le Chef du Service de la Population Blanche ..à .Elisabethville...............
Het Hoofd van de Dienst der Blanke Bevolking te
certifie que : — *verklaart dat :*
1° Mme .... née le — *geboren de* .... à — *te* ....
          est l'épouse de M^r ....
          de echtgenote is van de heer
2° le(s) enfant(s) mineur(s) ci-après :
     het/de minderjarige onderstaande kind/kinderen
.Albert........................, né (e) le — *geboren de* ...26.2.1943...............

fait/font partie de la famille de ...Monsieur .RUSSO, .Moïse............. ..
deel uitmaakt/maken van het gezin van
qui réside dans le Territoire de ..Elisabethville......... et ..(réf ..)
die verblijft in het Gewest   *en houder is van*
du certificat de résidant permanent n° ..I/82.........délivré en date du ....21.mars .1950...............
het bewijs van permanent resident nr.   *afgegeven op*
par (la Province ..du .Katanga................................
    (*de Provincie*
door(le Service de la Colonisation du Gouvernement Général
    (*de Kolonisatiedienst van het Gouvernement Generaal*

Elle/il (s) est/sont autorisé (e/s) à pénétrer sur le Territoire de la Colonie, muni (e/s) uniquement de pièces
d'identité et de certificats de vaccination encore valides.
Zij/hij is/zijn gemachtigd op het grondgebied van de Kolonie binnen te komen voorzien van hun identiteits-
stukken en geldige inentingsbewijzen.
(Biffer les mentions inutiles.)   Elisabethville.. le — de .2 .juillet... 1953.
(*Het overbodige doorhalen.*)   (Signature : — *Handtekening :*)   F. Bivort,

Enregistrer et codifier
Tamponner et classer
L'administration rêve

The mail a man of letters receives
After it has been written
a story lives its own life

The
Chicago Tribune
NELSON ALGREN
AWARDS
for short fiction

Thank you for allowing us to consider your short story
for The Nelson Algren Awards. Although your submission
did not win, we wish you good luck and many future
successes.

The Chicago Tribune   1990
Nelson Algren Awards Committee

All 3 of these stories
are very well-written —
"Diary" is imaginative,
as is "Glas Rost" —
the "Marina" story is
best, sensitive &
haunting — should make
it into print —
Good work!

435 NORTH MICHIGAN AVENUE   CHICAGO, ILLINOIS 60611

the volcano review
peninhand press
142 Sutter Creek Canyon
Volcano, California 95689
For the hometown in you...

"Your son, Leopold" by Albert Russo
has been awarded a prize of $75.00 as the
best story in an international "long fiction"
contest held by The Volcano Review, a
small press literary and arts magazine, and
sponsored by the National Endowment for
the Arts, and will be published in the forth-
coming book, "All Stories, All Kinds."

Tom Janisse
Editor & Publisher

ALBERT RUSSO
B.P. 640
75826 PARIS CEDEX 17
France

Le courrier d'un homme de lettres
Après avoir été écrite
une histoire vit sa vie

Such a peaceful place
How I'd like to stay here forever
still-life in an abolished time

Un endroit paisible
J'aimerais y rester à jamais
nature morte dans un temps aboli

Such a peaceful place
but I wouldn't like to stay here for long
this is a crocodile farm

Un endroit paisible
Je n'aimerais cependant y rester pour rien au monde
C'est une ferme à crocodiles

A Mercury Stratocruiser for a ride
a Peugeot 404 for work
Sweet sound of engines!

Une Mercury Stratocruiser pour la promenade
une Peugeot 404 pour le travail
Doux ronronnement des moteurs!

Capetown, by the sea
A lovely day
Premise of the anti-apartheid novel: Le Cap Des Illusions

Le Cap, au bord de la mer
Un jour superbe
Prémisse du roman anti-apartheid: Le Cap Des Illusions

The adult to come
is a dream in every kid's mind
"When I'm a grown up, I'll be a…"

L'adulte à venir
est un rêve pour les enfants
"Quand je serai grand, je serai un…"

In every adult mind
a child refuses to die
longing for his time of innocence

Dans l'esprit de chaque adulte
un enfant refuse de disparaître
regrettant le temps de l'innocence

To create is a question of patience
A masterpiece requires talent,
obstinacy ... and that touch of magic

Créer est une question de patience
Un chef-d'œuvre demande du talent,
de l'obstination ... et cette touche de magie

Why don't you give me a call?
It's so simple
Just ask for the spider in its web

www.bn.com

 cart   account   help   order

Home | **Bookstore** | Out of Print | College Textbooks | Bargain Books | eBooks | Articles for Download | Music | DVD& Video | PC & Video Games | Magazine Subscriptions | Online Course

Browse Subjects   Kids   New Releases   Bestsellers   Coming Soon

 QUICK SEARCH [Keyword ▼] [   ] [SEARCH] ADVANCED SEARCH

Book Search Results

We found **19** titles from author **albert russo**.

▶ More titles from our network of out of print book dealers from author **albert russo.**

Below are 1 - 19 of the 19 titles sorted in **bestselling order**.

Re-sort this list in [A-Z by Title] or [Publication Date] order.

1. **Zany:** Zapinette New York
In Stock:Ships within 24 hours .
Albert Russo / Hardcover /
Domhan Books / December 2000
Our Price: $17.95
[Add to Cart]

2. **The Age of the Pearl**
In Stock:Ships within 24 hours .
Albert Russo,Preface by Martin
Tucker / Paperback / Domhan
Books / December 2000
Our Price: $13.95
[Add to Cart]

3. **Albert Russo**
Albert Russo / Paperback / Europa
Media, Incorporated / July 1987
This title is not presently stocked by Barnes & Noble. Check availability from our network of book dealers.

4. **Beyond the Great Water**
In Stock:Ships within 24 hours .
Albert Russo,Preface by Martin A.
Tucker / Hardcover / Domhan
Books / December 2000
Our Price: $18.95
[Add to Cart]

5. **Beyond the Great Water**
In Stock:Ships within 24 hours .
Albert Russo,Preface by Martin
Tucker / Paperback / Domhan
[Add to Cart]

 Your Shopping Cart

No items in cart.
Go To Checkout

FREE Shipping

- **Same low prices as always!**
- **Buy two or more items to qualify.**
  See Details

Back to search page

◼ Search Other Areas

Find **albert russo** in

- Bargain
- eBooks
- Prints and Posters
- Music
- Reader's Catalog Recommendations
- Northern Light article archive
- Video
- College Textbooks

Pourquoi ne viendriez-vous pas me voir?
C'est si facile
Demandez l'araignée dans sa toile

Sometimes, someone comes
and soothes our solitude
Something to cherish and protect

Quelquefois, quelqu'un vient
qui brise notre solitude
Quelque chose à chérir et protéger

Somewhere, in our crowded world,
somebody cares
A feeling to savor like a God-given gift

Quelque part dans notre monde surpeuplé
savoir que quelqu'un pense à vous
Une émotion à savourer comme un don du ciel

Thousands of words
Thousands of pages
Just one life

Des milliers de mots
Des milliers de pages
Une seule vie

Printed in the United States
By Bookmasters